Behind

The

Darkness

Poetry from a mind

By Les Gardonyi

Printed in the United States of America
Gardonyi Poems Publisher: Self Publishing Inc.
51 East 42nd Street, New York, NY 10017

Contents

Contents

Dedication

*With love to my family, Judy, Adam, Melissa, Arie
and all those related to us through either genetics,
marriage or friendship*

Memento Mori

*Erno, Ilona, Emilia, Fulop, Annuska, Julo, Lajos,
Miklos, Lili, Andor, Gyuri, Peti, Ica, Sanyi, Gyuszi,
Joska, Marton, Julianna, Jeno, Pista*

1st poem I heard from my mother

*En Istenem, jo Istenem —lecsukodik mar a szemem,
de a Tied nyitva Atyam, amig alszom vigyaz ream.
Vigyaz kedves szuleimre, meg az en jo
hozzatartozoimra —hogy mikor a nap ujra felkel,
csokolhassuk egymast reggel. Amen…*

Introduction

A mind... perhaps my mind.

Back in the early 1980's I attended a school that taught us it was all "one mind". I didn't understand what that meant at the time but the school also taught us how to develop our powers of observation. And with that power we became more aware of our respective life experiences; how similar they were and yet each one of us expressing them differently. Poetry is a form of this observation-exercise that allows us to meet behind the darkness of confusion and share in the unifying impressions of a single mind.

-L.G.

Prologue

Sometime, between her years of high school and college, a talented friend of my daughter visited us and sketched the picture that is now on the cover of this book. The resulting image was immediately striking and the family realized that it had an alluring quality about it. Eventually it became my muse and I began to delve into what the image might try to convey. I freed up my mind and from this meditation came a number of poems in this book. Other inspirations came from direct experience as a result of riding this planet over sixty times around our sun.

A Portrait by Danielle

She saw it just then...
Behind, through, within her
That shimmer surrounding
Darkness, still and void

Raising her face
To brightness streaming
Passing, shining from somewhere
Now seen –now felt
Draws her stare there

And in that instant
The figure of a girl
Created on paper
Transcends black and white
To remain forever transfixed –a work of art

Face of Youth

It's the face of youth
Slightly turned from shadow to light
The beginning of knowledge
As though another birth had occurred
From the 17th year hence

How very questioning of life-
What is this light
That shows the way for my new truth?
I am older, wiser, less fragile
Out of the old darkness I do emerge

It is exciting -yet I am calm
I know my presence —here, now
Looking up —I will look higher
Later at other ages —maturity
When into darkness one must gaze deeper still

Behind the Darkness

Swirls of darkness surround her head
In the depths of her lineage
Shades of grays are not permitted

A mother born in Czechoslovakia*
A father born in Hungary –
Oppressed lands created
For predestined refugees

Children born of parents who in turn
Suffered greatly from cruelty and hatred
In the death camps of the wars...

Such a darkness gives no compromise –
No capitulation for shading the mind
Only the emergence of pure white light
And she is the survivor

*Czechoslovakia existed in central-Europe from 1918 to 1992, and separated into Slovakia and the Czech Republic in 1993. The lands of Hungary were disected after WW I with the Treaty of Trianon. The inhabitants of the original land still live on the borders of the adjacent countries.

Life Decisions

Every age has a moment of choice
The road leads left or right, up or down,
dark or light...
Towards clarity —but mostly toward
confusion

Elevating thoughts of fanciful insights
None of which allow reality to form
Always the outcome different from the
intent

Why deliberate a choice?
It will make its own!
And one can follow without knowing where
it leads

This Age –My Age

In the nursing home
I saw many of the elderly
Seeing my future in me

As they spoke of their lives
And told of things that passed
It was really their present
Enduring their past

So difficult for some
To part with their history
Trading-in their memories
For a moment of recognition:

I was... I had...
I did... I said...

Sad recollections of bygone existences
They live on in a flood of
"Why-did-it have-to end?
How-can-I-get-it-back?
Why-can't-I-still-be-young... like you?"

And I know from them what I now have
This age that would otherwise become
Part of my old-age-ponderings as well

Momentary Musings of a Young Girl

How often I have looked there
And seen nothing in particular-
Yet gazed as recollections and fantasies
appeared...

Once the thought of a boy
With long blond hair-
We shared sweet moments in each other's arms

And then also, there was the fight with the family
Dad or Mom... or my brother-
I should have said... and I should have done... and
didn't

Now it's the piano recital that played
Flawlessly from key to key, note to note-
The sounds repeating perfectly, again and again

Out of the mists of my mind
Appear scenarios I might have been a part of-
Or yet plan to be

Then I stare and see
What others can't-
Because this is MY light shining through MY eyes
Ever captured and freed by reality's whim

I Read Some Books

I read some books that were
Not along my lines of thoughts
They spoke of religion and ways
That I did not espouse

But I read them to my self
And realized their truth
As the vapor of the words
Soaked through my dry soul

Leaving me less parched
On the open seas
That had been stagnant
Within my cavernous being

And so I understand and
See a little more than before
As looking in and looking out
I find myself again

Speaking

And speaking of sex
I told my friends
I knew of its powers
And they wanted to know more

The more I spoke
The less I knew
As though each sound
Was stealing an intimate breath

So I stopped speaking
And felt its strength return
As though silence was knowledge
Not hidden —but sensed

Loneliness

I'm always with my self
How can I be lonely?
As friends we met often-
But intimacy kept us apart

How close can I get?
How much can I know...
Before I become frightened
Of newer knowledge
Glinting in the eye of my last reflection

From depths unfathomed
I've surfaced a familiar stranger
To be met yet again
By that simple stable part of me
I know only as truth

Traveling to Know

That's it then –I'm going!

My studies must continue
In the land of my ancestors
All these history-things I've learned here
Must now morphing-shape take there
Become real and tangible experiences
Embedded in my life's core
All the more, more and ever more

It all comes so easily –once you decide.

Travel-fare, and clothing
Well-wishes and flight
Through the clouds and through the night
I arrive more aware of my intent
For a second chance at Jerusalem

My youth so young at 14 to really know
I could only sense this space... for then
I could only tourist-travel... ago
I could only food-taste and sight-see... before
I could only hello-say... to others
I could not really myself-be

6 years later life is fairer
Bringing me along to favor...
How I've been prepared, been taught
Been accepted, been shunned
Been special, been anonymous
Been worked, been rested
Been loved and created
For this essential moment of hereness

Pulled by Clotho
Measured by Lachesis and cut by Atropos...
I will let this year circle ever so slowly
Back into time's fishing reel
For I will have been caught only
For a short time struggling
To return to life's main stream
Toward a different lure.

Two Students / One Room

We're two students in a single room
Sharing only a moment in the present
With futures diverging too fast
And both powerless to slow its effects

Who is she, I wonder many times
What is she really like
When I am not a part of her space
When neither of us really cares

Last year when we met
She was already aloof and distant
She brought into the room her yellow bike
And hung it in the closet and quickly left

Later we decorated our respective spaces
A picture here a flower there
Perhaps a rug for the cold floor's influence
And simple words to keep our distance

She was pretty and had a boyfriend
Liked sports and active places
I am pretty and have a boyfriend
Like my comfort and quiet gazes

We parted silently in the middle
Of the second year
She moved out without much flair
Left unannounced for me to care

And my room is mine now
The sole occupant of this time —of this space
There is no one to share with, a muted violence
Only to decorate it completely with my silence

Next Week

A man embracing God,
He comes once a week
Reintroducing his eternal mate
To my brother, my mother, my father and me

We greet Them
We wash hands
We pray
We learn
We speak
We part

I understand more now –
Until next week,
When my stale thoughts
Will again be refreshed

A Prayer

Dear God I know You're always around
But I don't always notice You.
It seems that unless there is a crisis or some
sentimental occasion,
It is difficult to pay attention to you

I live in a world that is constantly drawing
my attention toward its chaotic activities-
When I am involved with the world in this
way I lose my thoughts of You
I become separated from You and I am left
fragmented.

A piece of me becomes a son,
Another piece of me, a husband
And other pieces identify themselves as a
father, a job-function...
And even the illusion of being this body.

I am forever dreaming and imagining
And re-living moments that may or may not
have existed.
In this tumult of thoughts and roles,
I need to feel stillness!

A stillness that reunites my sense of self,
A stillness that subsides all activities,
A stillness that comes when my thoughts
drift to You
And I notice You —again.

Grandma's Doctor

Hello... hello Mari?
Yeh... so I went to the doctor
I tell him I have some pains
In my shoulders – in my arms – in my legs
He looks close and he says

"Can I bring in my assistant
He's just starting out...?"
And this young man came in
But he was a good looking Jewish guy
And he said, "Hi"

And I was looking at his yamika
And I never saw such a beautiful Jewish guy
Him, I had to meet
And I asked him how old are you young man
He says "27... can I see your feet?"
Said... I have a girl for you, it's my granddaughter
Says he..."I'm married" –Ahhh, but did he have a brother

So Mari... I'm OK
Just some arthritis in my bones today
But that young doctor was a treat to see
And he made the pain go away... for free

Somewhere Out There

Somewhere out there...
There's land where
Green grass grazes
Cows and tall
Trees block small streams-

Somewhere out there's
A house in a wilderness
Some mad dreamer abandoned to rot!
No one claims its home
Just the memory of time-

Somewhere out there
A pretty girl gets wasted
In the tumult of maturity
Her beauty turns inward
While her splendor spreads out-

Somewhere out there
A moneyman drops his income
On the roulette wheel of life...
His ball of fortune so
Matter-of-factly takes flight-

Somewhere out there
So many things occur that
I would gladly accept
Whereas others would not-

Somewhere out there
A balloon expands and the spiral climbs-
And they'll never collapse
For somewhere out there...
Is in here, perhaps

Attempting to Meditate

...one, one, one, one, one...
-And the second partial can be integrated to-

...one, one, one, one, one...
-Her looks are coming closer, she's taking off the top of-

...one, one, one, one, one...
-My subconscious is really a non-dimensional entity sliding to the surface of my consciousness at times, but when I wish to recall how I did it –I just don't seem able to, and frustration overtakes my attempts-

...one, one, one, one, one...
-breathe in, breathe out-

...one, one, one, one, one...
-She's naked now and reaching for me, I see her hand move towards my-

...one, one, one, one, one...
-The other side of the galaxy is much more livelier than our-

...one, one, one, one, one...
-My parents are missing me, what if something should happen to them, what if-

...one, one, one, one, one...
-My principle of magnetic levitation is a
private success and I can fly above the earth's
cities, I can visit them all at this enormous
speed which I am able to-

...one, one, one, one, one...
-I am one with the galaxy, with the universe,
with my plant, with my unreachable-

...one, one, one, one, one...
-She's pregnant and I am too, we share our
love 'till eternity's-

...one, one, one, one, one...
-Will I be a father of meaningful experience to-

...one, one, one, one, one...
-Old man in the cave, though you appear, I do
not attempt to query all my problems from
you —me-

...one, one, one, one, one...
-Levitation is so simple, and my surroundings
are able to be spun with ease, I can tumble
through this space of-

...one, one, one, one, one...
-And why shouldn't I just rise through the ranks to the top; or why shouldn't I just turn into the gray mouse, unnoticed, oscillating between the two –without time for-

...one, one, one, one, one...
-A statuesque female figure –it's made of golden

...one, one, one, one, one...
-But so what if I know the future; and there is no past, alas, only the present changes into-

...one, one, one, one, one...

Transcendence

LIFE EXISTS ON THE EARTH,
WE ALL KNOW THAT BY NOW,
IT'S BEEN LONG AGO,
THE COSMOS KNOW THAT
LIFE EXISTS HERE NOW

LIFE EXISTS ON THE MOON,
WE ALL KNOW THAT BY NOW,
IT'S BEEN LONG AGO,
GURDJIEFF FORESAW
LIFE EXISTS THERE NOW

LIFE EXISTS IN THE MIND OF GOD,
WE ALL KNOW THAT BY NOW,
IT'S BEEN LONG AGO,
THE HEAVENS KNOW THAT
LIFE EXISTS IN NOW

The 23rd

The 23rd approaches to moment the occasion
The calendar abides without anticipation
I'm 23 for USA
To underline my Epoch Day

For in that era I had come
From a land where crowds did hum
"On your feet, your homeland calls you!
Now or never, slavery won't do!"

But this to me was fabulous
The mobs I passed were nebulous
They shook, they shoved, they knew they'd matter
Through the bodies I would scatter

Ran the streets straight down the lane
Home to parents' arms I came
Then we heard the guns roar out
The bullets found their well-lit route

We grabbed our clothes and ran away
Through the thickets, guards and hay
And while all this had come about
I knew nothing –but had my doubts

My reality was formed for me
By the other twenty-three
The story they had shaped so big
Was "...traveling to feast a pig!"

Moments passed into the days
Calm acceptance in my brains
For once we cleared across the line
My father's visions now were mine

Revelations from his lips
Related why we made the trips
We came away from darkness then
Light began to shine again

I knew a truth in that set moment
Yet felt the same unshaken torment
Why did I not yell out loud
A cheer so great to wake the crowd

How could I remain so cold
Unfazed yet aware and bold
I acknowledged what I learned
From my father's lips concerned

His hopes had now been rearranged
By my mother's will deranged
For it was she who forced our choices
Made in mandatory voices

An ultimatum stressed with pain
N'er again to slavery's chain
Shackled with a senseless guilt
That six million had to quit

And so we rambled 'cross the plain
'Till a car stopped by to halt our bane
Ironic language that we knew
Could shelter refugees anew

The 23rd had passed away
And took with it another day
A day we knew would come again
When our future there began

Survival

I am here and
       I will stay
I exist-
       I know the way
I will eat all
       That is offered
I will drink
       When all have sobered
I will see the world
       Evolve
I can think my
       Mind to solve
I'm the one,
       I am the all
I can stand and
       Never fall
I'm the source and
       I'm the sink
I'm the start whose
       End can't link
I am at last afraid
       To see
I am all that
       Threatens me

On the Subway

How to look?

Should I have a vacuous look on my face-
And not draw any attention to myself?
Or should IT be one of self-inflicted contortions,
Satisfying some internal desires for impatience's
movements?

The blank look works for some of the book-
readers
As they shift their feet –
One to the front, one to the back
Trying not to bump knees with those sitting next
to them.
But contact of some form is inevitable.

A mother carrying a sleeping baby,
Conversing with her in another language-
It doesn't matter what is being said,
Only the emotion.

There's one sitting with radio-plugs in the ear-
Leans back and lets the loud sounds
Seep deep within a silent brain...
Why think? Why react? Let IT live for me.

Such a pretty face,
Gazing straight ahead
Trying not to notice all the intentional stares.
The look of defense —a sense of insecurity.

Hunched over in sleepless rest,
A bum shrivels in the corner.
Hands half-inside his pants and...
Holds whatever he's got left.
He's always looking away.

Pratt Student Lounge 1972

Sitting in the student lounge
Morning sun shines on my mind
Music beats the student air
Students sleeping without care

Open book –blank look
Confused eyes –dizzy "Hi!"s
Fast paced steps…
Nowhere friends

"Chess?"
"…K!"
"Card?"
"Hey!"
Conversations without flare

Time leads
Man feeds
Sun climbs
Mind winds

Pawn moves, knight jumps
Bishops rush and head numbs
"One more?" – "Why not?!"
Cut the class; term shot

Sun is high and really bright
Room is getting very hot
Sweater's off on top of books
People giving heavy looks

One whole wall is window space
Students pacing in their place
Music sets their varied gait
With a mark that seals their fate

Blank stares are the norm for some
Inspiration for some fun
Artists sketch their still-life prey
Pretty girls with shallow play

Engineers will slide their rules
Equating some abstract tools
Tools of trade no one will bare
For once he's out —no one will care

Conflicts here are rarely seen
Peace will dominate the scene
The restless peace that isolates
Lonely people wanting mates

Time lags,
Man sags,
Sun sets,
Mind ends...

The Riddle of the Middle

I'm always in the middle of history
No matter how long I've existed in time-
My present bisects all that was
From the other half that's yet to mime.

Why?

Because my HERE is forever between

...beginning and end
...oblivion and eternity
...seen and will see

But where I am now is neverafter
And neverbefore is yet to be

Talking to the Night

In quiescent moments of drifting gray
Recumbent on a gradual sway

I sit inclined to speak out fair
Toward water droplets in the air

My breath forms subtly, mixing brusquely
Reformed mists swirl through about me

Thoughts are begged to form the sounds
From the ghosts that passed my bounds

Such a night must never end
Without a link to round the bend

Now I stand and walk within
The narrow path that must begin

Searching through my soul with whispers
Nighttime's darkness clearly hinders

Yet I force the tones aloud
But no one hears the groaning clouds

The blackness captures all the moans
Leaving only muted OMs

A Mystical Mistake

As I spoke a quiet tone
My mind wondered outside this zone
Toward oblivion's unknown
...and it was at this point where I blundered

For uncertain memories roam
Unbounded by will alone
That led me to a steady drone
...when again I may have faltered

Lost my self in marvels –laden with autonomy
Swirling amidst the torrents of lofty astronomy
I hung in the balance between Exodus and
Deuteronomy
...defying creation with my malaise

Having fallen back to time
Sinking senses sift sublime
Upon the tones I traveled through a line of
prayer
...in a flash of ecstasy I saw my mistake much
clearer

Thus I embraced and accepted with patience
Lifelong habits renounced as donations
An abstinence of atonements for previous
incarnations
...then I remained stable, still and silent

My Father's Arm on my Shoulder

It's a kind of weight you don't mind bearing
A welcome burden laden with pride
A gentle, honest and sincere load
Pressing reliance into my hide

How he stands towering above me
Ageless, fearless, tied to his prime
A hunter-gatherer-survivor and savior
Always knowing his arms will be mine

Drawn into his life through this hand on my side
No times can depart us, no ties can unbind
Linked now forever though in age we did part
I love you dear father –your arm's in my heart

Playing Peek-a-boo with God

As a child, from my third-floor window across
the barrier's divide
I saw a teenage girl's eyes peep through some
curtained lights
When she hid –I looked
When she looked –I hid
She smiled, a glint of friendship hints

Many years later, I looked up at some clouds
And saw the sun hiding more often than not
When it hid -I looked
When it shined –I hid
We're setting and rising at eternity's bid

From births to deaths I cycle through
Peeking past at me and You
When You hide –I seek
When You look –I know
Together we find no barriers grow

Solar Messiah in M-87

Glowing at the center of a symbiotic universe
Where each entity grew from an internal
source
XT@Q made contact with its neighbor D#N&

Together they exchanged nothing but
acknowledgement
As the others joined in: "We must help... there
is a problem..."
Was the emanated sensation perceived by all-

"There is fragmentation from LOCU$9..."
It continued with the alarming news-
"We must summon the ultimate uniter..."
It grieved on-

"We must allow 'sharing' this time!"
All agreed, and at that moment
It came into being...
The Solar Messiah in M-87

Ageing

The shaking hands
Out held these sands
Of time renounced
To bend the ends

The thinning hair
To mirror's care
Reflects the age
These two can share

The lines remain
Upon the plane
Expressing gestures
Sought in vain

The wrinkled years
The mounting fears
Prove youth's folly
No longer nears

Memories grieved
Through the brain sieved
Separates out
The past we weaved

The onward goal
To reach the pole
Demands are made
To play the role

The stick is pulled
The lines are ruled
To measure out
How much we're fooled

To time our sands
The bottle bends
We turn the glass
With shaking hands

Adam 4, Melissa 1

There, in the other end of the room
He approaches swiftly-
Eyes now meet with breath out flowing
Touch – a burst of smile is looming

And they gaze for so long
Into mirrors of reflecting rapport
There is no break in their tense
What do they sense that prolongs their trance

What extra light do they ray
Into one another's bosom they pray
Which, holding tight –yet apart still it joins
The brother/sister bond there forms

Haiku #1

Sympathy's flower
Falls petals upon other
Flower's empty stem

Doodling* Manias

Riding north on the Palisades, they-it stand so bold with branches old and broken but secured by common roots, that I can't help but remark as I pass the mystic moment –"There's Three Trees"

Contemplating thoughts that boil my mental oils –frustration hones my canines as they carve into my lips the image of the Halloween prostheses which I once had bought... "Four Teeth"

My pen in idle scribbling will begin to draw a shape who's origins I can't locate but its haunting presence always appears upon the paper and its most important attribute must critically be placed lest I continue to replace with single strokes I make the... "Double M's"

The lines must form and reform as they must head toward a goal; there is no haphazardness; there is no coincidence; there is only accidental chance –they must all... "Converge"

Rest must follow frenzy but the aim is still the same —the circles are concentric and the goal is to remain in the center of the... "Bull's Eye"

Cross the lines from left and right, up and down and in and out —elaboration bears a fruit that ripens with a purposeful resolve —to captivate a... "Star"

But now to escape to a fanciful allure —toward a never-ending style that though repetitious, evolves into a rule to... "Loop de Loop"

Then rebuild the Universe with orderly spots — building up their reason by stacking the... "Dots"

Why do they shrink and how do they expand — the cyclic lines are so undulatingly fascinating as my comprehension... "Zigzags"

Which way will I go now —where can I start to continue again —what is their meaning and why must I express them; these symbols that point me toward my realm with archetypal... "Arrows"

*I'm certain that some of these doodles (see p. 8) are common to many of us. A kind of Jungian set of archytypes – expressions of some shared memories. Reminders... to re-mind.

Doubt

"Such little faith in moral bait
Keep fishes in water -never getting smarter"

Give me proof of it all!
Show me what really IS.

I drift through life suspecting
Never knowing for sure...
What people think -opinions
When people do -intentions
Where I should be -purpose
Why I can't know -truth

Let the totality of eternity
Play through my mind's sanity
To rest these emotions finally
About uncertainty's duality

Foolish Minds

Minds of fools
Shape clever tools
To carve away
At truth's array

While manic minds
Will undermine
The sanctity
Of clarity

Layed Off

"Reduction in force" says the morning paper,
"Reduction in force" says the boss,
"Reduction in force" says the hired fire-er
"Reduction in force" says I to my family

"It's the economy" says the TV,
"It's the economy" says the internet,
"It's the economy" says my head-hunter agent
"It's the lies" says I to myself

Reduction

...And where after all did this floor come from
Beginning, creation, invention, construction, evolution

...Are we not after all human
Cell, fish, frog, ape, man

...Are we not after all
History, destiny, fate

...Are we not
Negation, destruction

...Are we
Existence

...Are
Being

...A
Simplification, unity

...

Dissociation

When I used to smoke

Sucking on my cigarette
I taste the bitter weed-
And while I feel no 'regrette'
My mind will plant a seed

It is fertilized by the smoke
Of the glowing red dot-
My fingers slowly stroke
As the cylinder gets hot

Why do I masturbate
A rolled piece of paper-
Why do I rotate
This illusion of flavor

The effluvium drifts by
And with my thoughts it disappears-
Blankness in my eyes
Silence in my ears

I breathe in the small pieces
Of burned residue-
And the feeling in my head eases
For the euphoria that's due

As I gaze in the distant
Life I've drifted through
My thoughts will run rampant
Over my colored actions' hue

Where have I been
And what have I done
What have I seen
And was it all fun

Questions...
Questions I will never truly answer
Conceptions...
Conceived in empty anger

Ah... rebellion against purpose
A – way to throw a rock-
The formidable service
Outdone by the clock

Futility exhales my thoughts
Blue smoke exits without-
Change has altered all its faults
Nothing exists throughout

The ashes have formed
And its length is consumed-
A memory is mourned
Its past is assumed

My flick of the wrist
Propels the smoldering embers-
They explode in a mist of sentiments
Which no one remembers

After Birth

Look how little formed so fresh
Clings upon her bosom's flesh

Mother's milk so suckling sweet
Trickles to her sucking beat

Eyes still shut to still the world
Heartbeats were the sounds she heard

In that darkness born of mirth
Floating in the liquid earth

Then she grew to push a grudge
From within her mother's bulge

And so upon the unknown date
Arrived to bare her naked fate

Awaiting life to fill her soul
Came prepared to play her role

In her eyes are drifting blue
She sleeps —the hours change their hue

And in her dreams she smiles at me
Awaiting life's maturity

A Higher Force

How does it enter?
Through the top of the head
Down the spine
Below the sphincter
Into the belly-
A round ball of being exists within

What is its purpose?
The mind directs it
Through bones and viscera
Circulates it through intelligencia
Feeds it to the earth-
In humble repose and leaves

Where has it gone?
Left to search for another
Without a host it wanders
Creating sparks it hovers
Waiting for one to stay still

Ah! There... Whooooooosh

A 9/11 STOP!

Flipped a page in the "Masters of Wisdom"*
When the subway stopped amid reason
Above, the sirens sang and lured
Me out of comfort quietly cured

Arising from the traveled cave
My eyes beheld a static blaze
I in shadow, they in sun
Burning towers... gashed... undone!

Slowly I began my trek
Toward the place my work should stack
A camera from my sack would click
People falling –dying quick

Then someone yelled at me to run
I heard a rushing sound begun
An avalanche was clouding toward me
The thought of dying struck me quickly

Running down an esplanade
I hid inside a restaurant
While the dust blows past this cage
So does wisdom from the masters' page

*"The Masters of Wisdom" – book written by J.G. Bennet.

Mars Time

A crimson orb spinning slower than Earth
Evolving its rocks without any birth
Pockmarked with craters through the millennia
Revealing its dust above Elysium Planitia

An earthly spirit surrounded by halos
Hangs from red skies on a space platform's gallows
Bounces to the surface imprinting its stain
Sol-1 begins on the Gusev Plain

Rocks of ages loom in the distance
Samples of permanence meeting resistance
Deus ex-machina, impersonal and pushy
Tagging its targets "Adirondack" and "Sushi"

At latitude North and longitude East
A kin to the spirit's opportunistic feast
It drops straight down into Meridiani Planum
A mysterious colony of rocks ridicules its sanctum

Winds are howling throughout this ancient place
Dust devils haunt and carve an eerie face
Its beauty and sanctity so quickly undone
Now the universe learns the invasion's begun

Ode to Rossolimo

Sweet Caissa* can you find
The magic in my master's mind
You inspire all the thought
Brilliancy has brought forth

With what might would you desire
Intellect to burn its fire
Ashes now are all remains
Of the bulk that once was brains

How you hovered o'er the ken
When there moved –those wooden men
Lighted with agility
Upon checkered reality

Taken now from off this ball
Taken with a planless fall
No longer to start again
With life's little wooden men

Oh Caissa can you claim
Eternity for all its fame
Life remains upon the board
O'er which no one's ever lord

*Caissa – mythical goddess/muse of chess

Is this the Last

As the earth moves through its solstice cycle
Tipping angles toward the minus
Summer travels through the lines
Shifting sunlight toward new climes
When did it happen...
That last day of summer?

(In the momentum of joys
We never anticipate transitions
A simple turn of reflection
On a less-than-perfect moment
And we know...
A season has passed)

I was watching so closely in mid-winter
At the last moments of sunlight's glimmer
The shortest days contract with motions
Burdened feelings strip our notions
Lost in thought we bring demise
To the awareness of the last days of our lives

Afterword

An instructor of movements, Mme. J. DeSalzmann, once remarked that our life has a pattern and that we don't see it immediately – but little by little it begins to show. The poetry I've written has provided a few dots to connect –resulting in a unique glimpse at that pattern.

It's a pattern that can be recognized through an extra-dimensional perspective. One which will result in a kind of a map. My intention is to leave this "map of poetry" behind for those who want to journey along a similar labyrinthine path.

And why travel this path at all?
What, after all, is the goal?

A martial artist friend of mine responded with the following Chinese characters...

押
忍
中
庸
之
道

www.ingramcontent.com/pod-product-compliance
Lightning Source LLC
Chambersburg PA
CBHW060716030426
42337CB00017B/2881